a *factastic* tour

A IS FOR
AUSTRALIA

Frané Lessac

WALKER BOOKS
AND SUBSIDIARIES
LONDON • BOSTON • SYDNEY • AUCKLAND

Australia is packed with amazing places to discover – from the outback to ancient rainforests, the Snowy Mountains, the Great Barrier Reef and more.

The mainland is the largest island on Earth and also the smallest continent.

Exmouth

Western Australia (WA)

Much of Australia is covered by remote areas, where only a few people live, called "the outback".

Fremantle

Rottnest Island

Yallingup

Valley of the Giants

Over 8000 islands make up the country.

Australia is similar in size to the USA. Great Britain fits into Australia 33⅓ times.

Australia is nicknamed "Down Under" because it's below many other countries and looks like it's at the bottom of the globe.

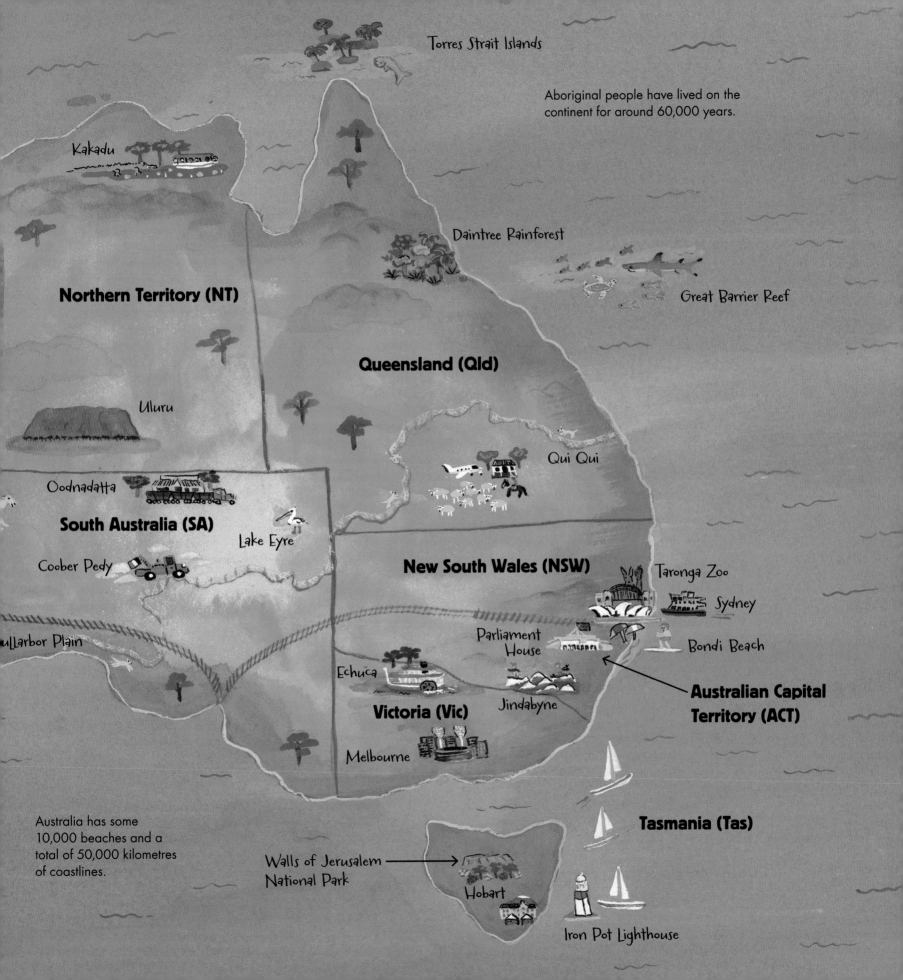

Torres Strait Islands

Aboriginal people have lived on the continent for around 60,000 years.

Kakadu

Daintree Rainforest

Northern Territory (NT)

Great Barrier Reef

Queensland (Qld)

Uluru

Qui Qui

Oodnadatta

South Australia (SA)

Lake Eyre

Coober Pedy

New South Wales (NSW)

Taronga Zoo

Sydney

Parliament House

Bondi Beach

Nullarbor Plain

Australian Capital Territory (ACT)

Echuca

Victoria (Vic)

Jindabyne

Melbourne

Australia has some 10,000 beaches and a total of 50,000 kilometres of coastlines.

Tasmania (Tas)

Walls of Jerusalem National Park

Hobart

Iron Pot Lighthouse

Bondi Beach (NSW) is Australia's most famous beach for swimming, surfing and sunbathing.

The red and yellow lifesavers' flags show you where it's safe to swim.

Surf lifesavers wear caps that are the colours of the nautical flag for "man overboard". One of the first lifesaving clubs in the world was started at Bondi Beach.

The Festival of the Winds at Bondi is Australia's largest kite festival.

The Bondi to Coogee coastal walk is a great way to view the beautiful beaches and bays of Sydney.

Until the early 1900s, swimming at Bondi was banned between 9 am and 8 pm. Men and women were never allowed to swim together, as it was considered indecent – even with women wearing neck-to-knee bathing attire.

Since records began there have been around 800 shark attacks in Australia.

An underwater shark net is located a few hundred metres off the beach to protect swimmers.

Coober Pedy (SA) is the largest opal mining area in the world.

Looking for opals in rock heaps is called "noodling".

Opals are natural gemstones that flash iridescent colours.

The first "tree" in the town was made from scrap iron.

The Antakirinja Matu-Yankunytjatjara people are the traditional owners of the land at Coober Pedy. Their word for the area is *kupa-piti*, which means "man who lives in a hole".

Golf is played in the cool of the night. Glowing golf balls are used and there's no grass. Golfers tee off from a small piece of "turf" they carry with them.

To escape the heat, some Coober Pedy residents live in underground caves called "dugouts". There are also underground hotels, museums, churches and even shops.

**D**

Daintree Rainforest (Qld)
is the largest rainforest in Australia
and the oldest on the planet.

The "idiot fruit" is one of the rarest flowering plants
on Earth. Found in the Daintree, its tennis-ball-sized
fruit have seeds that are extremely poisonous.

The trees are so densely packed that it can take up to 10 minutes for a single raindrop to reach the forest floor.

The traditional owners of the Daintree area are the Kuku Yalanji people.

The Daintree Rainforest is over 135 million years old.

Many snakes in the Daintree are venomous. The taipan's poison is one of the world's deadliest. The amethystine python can grow up to 8.5 metres long and kills its prey by suffocation.

Echuca (Vic) is a port on the Murray River and home to Australia's largest paddle-steamer fleet.

The world's biggest waterski race is held every year on the Murray River.

Echuca is a Yorta Yorta Aboriginal word meaning "meeting of the waters".

The PS *Adelaide* is one of the oldest working paddle-steamers in the world.

The Murray River is one of the longest navigable rivers in the world. It starts as a small stream near Australia's highest mountain, Mount Kosciuszko, and ends its journey at the mouth of the river in Goolwa, South Australia.

F

Fremantle (WA) is one of the best preserved 19th-century seaports in the world.

On summer nights, the harbour is crowded with people dining on fish and chips.

Early each morning fishing boats deliver their catch of rock lobsters, scallops and sardines caught in the Indian Ocean.

Fremantle is known as *Walyalup* by the Noongar people, the traditional owners of the land.

The Fremantle Doctor is a cool sea breeze that blows in from the ocean on hot summer days.

Once a year, Italian fisherman celebrate the Blessing of the Fleet by parading the statues of Our Lady of Martyrs and Madonna di Capo d'Orlando through the streets of Fremantle to the harbour.

Great Barrier Reef (Qld) is made up of around 900 islands and almost 3000 coral reefs.

On the reef there are approximately 2000 species of fish, 30 species of whales, 6 species of sea turtles, 125 species of sharks and stingrays, and 17 species of sea snakes.

The Great Barrier Reef can be seen from space and is one of the seven natural wonders of the world.

Some corals on the reef are nearly 500,000 years old.

Box jellyfish kill more people than snakes, sharks and crocodiles. Their sting is so poisonous that swimmers can die within minutes.

The reef has its own floating mailbox. You can mail a postcard with the world's only Great Barrier Reef stamp.

The crown-of-thorns starfish eats coral and is one of the biggest dangers to the reef.

Hobart is the capital of Tasmania, an island south of the Australian mainland.

The traditional owners of the land in which Hobart is located are the Muwinina people.

Snow-capped Mount Wellington towers above the city.

Hobart is known as Australia's gateway port to Antarctica.

On Saturdays, Salamanca Place comes alive with a colourful street market.

Iron Pot Lighthouse (Tas)
is the oldest original tower in Australia.

Originally fuelled by whale oil, it was the first lighthouse in Australia to be converted to solar power.

In 1862, one of the lighthouse keeper's children claimed to have found a gold nugget. Within hours the Iron Pot gold rush was on, but no further treasure was ever found.

The Sydney Hobart Yacht Race is an annual 628-nautical-mile race. It crosses the Bass Strait, which is famous for howling winds and wild seas. Once sailboats round the lighthouse, it's only 12 nautical miles to the finish line in Hobart.

Jindabyne (NSW) is the gateway to the ski fields of the Snowy Mountains.

Near Jindabyne is Mount Kosciuszko – the highest peak on the mainland at 2228 metres.

Snow gums have branches that can bend under the weight of heavy snow.

The largest engineering project ever undertaken in Australia is the Snowy Mountains Hydro-Electric Scheme. It channels water from the mountains through tunnels and dams to make electricity. Over 100,000 people from more than 35 countries worked on the project. This gathering of cultures is now seen as the beginning of multiculturalism in Australia.

Jindabyne's name comes from a
Monaro Ngarigo Aboriginal word
meaning "valley".

When the Snowy River was dammed as part of the Snowy
Mountains Hydro-Electric Scheme, the town of Jindabyne was
moved. What's left of the old town lies beneath Lake Jindabyne.

Kakadu (NT) is Australia's largest national park, covering nearly 20,000 square kilometres.

Saltwater crocodiles can grow up to 6 metres long and are the most dangerous reptiles on the planet. Their ancestors have been around since the time of the dinosaurs.

The word Kakadu comes from Gagadju, one of the local Aboriginal languages.

In the wetlands, you can spot tall jabiru birds and the jacana or Jesus bird. With its very long toes, the Jesus bird appears to walk on water as it spreads its weight on top of lily pads.

Kakadu has over 5000
Aboriginal rock art galleries.
Some paintings are more than
20,000 years old.

Barramundi are plentiful
in Kakadu. These fish start
life as males and at 4 to
5 years old, they change
and become females.

Australia does not have
alligators. The explorer
who named the West, East
and South Alligator Rivers
in Kakadu didn't know the
difference between an
alligator and a crocodile.

Lake Eyre (SA) is Australia's largest salt lake.

The lake is normally dry and has only filled completely 3 times in the last 150 years.

When water in the lake evaporates and salt levels increase, the lake looks pink.

About 6 to 8 million water birds from around the world travel thousands of kilometres to Lake Eyre when it is in flood.

When the lake floods the area comes alive with wildflowers and birdlife, fish and insects.

The name for Lake Eyre, given by the traditional owners, the Arabana people, is *Kati Thanda*.

According to Aboriginal legend, the Kudimudra is a bunyip-like creature that eats those who stray onto *Kati Thanda*.

The members of the Lake Eyre Yacht Club are a devoted group of people who wait patiently for the lake to flood so they can sail.

When full, Lake Eyre is actually 2 lakes connected by a channel.

Lake Eyre dragons are lizards that use body language to "talk" to each other. If they want to fight, mate, or simply travel across another lizard's territory, they let them know by waving their hands and bobbing up and down.

Melbourne is the capital city of Victoria and is also known as the sports capital of Australia.

Six light towers each hold 884 lamps and stand 75 metres high, equal to a 24-storey building.

Melbourne is located on the traditional land of the Kulin Nation.

The Melbourne Cricket Ground, known as "The G", can seat about 100,000 people and is famous for Australian rules football and cricket.

Melbourne was originally called Batmania, after John Batman, one of the city's founders.

Every year Victoria has a public holiday for a horse race called the Melbourne Cup, which is known as "the race that stops a nation".

In 1866, an all-Indigenous cricket team played at the Melbourne Cricket Ground, before touring England and becoming the first Australian sports team to compete overseas.

Nullarbor Plain is a flat, treeless area of Australia. Nullarbor comes from the Latin for nothing (*nullus*) and tree (*arbor*).

The Indian Pacific train travels along the world's longest stretch of straight track – 478 kilometres across the Nullarbor Plain.

The "dingo fence" is the longest fence in the world, at over 5300 kilometres in length. Its job is to stop dingoes from attacking sheep. It starts on the ocean cliffs of South Australia and continues all the way to Queensland.

The outback is home to the world's largest population of wild camels. The first camels were brought to Australia in the mid 1800s for transportation and exploration.

The Nullarbor is the largest limestone slab in the world, covering an area over 200,000 square kilometres.

The Nullarbor has one of the world's largest cave systems with over 250 caves.

Oodnadatta (SA) is a small outback town on the Oodnadatta Track, an ancient dirt trail used by Aboriginal people for thousands of years.

In the outback, the skies are so clear you can see thousands of stars. The best-known constellation is the Southern Cross, which is visible from anywhere in Australia and is used for navigation. It is so famous that its image appears on the Australian flag.

The name Oodnadatta is from the Arrernte Aboriginal word *Utnadata*, meaning "blossom of the mulga".

Road trains are trucks that pull extra trailers carrying livestock, fuel or minerals. The world record for the longest road train is 120 trailers.

At dawn and dusk, flocks of corellas, budgerigars, cockatoos and galahs gather at the springs along the track.

Parliament House (ACT) in the nation's capital, Canberra, is the meeting place of Australia's government.

Parliament House is located on the traditional lands of the Ngunnawal people.

The kangaroo and emu are represented on the Australian Coat of Arms. Since it is difficult for either animal to walk backwards, people say they symbolise a nation moving forwards.

The building houses the Senate, the House of Representatives and the offices of the Australian Prime Minister.

A mosaic floor made up of 90,000 granite pieces sits on an island in front of Parliament House. This artwork was designed by Michael Nelson Jagamara, an Aboriginal artist from the Northern Territory, and is based on his 1985 painting called *Possum and Wallaby Dreaming*.

The flag on top of Parliament House is as big as a double-decker bus. It takes 2 people to change it every 4 to 6 weeks.

The new Parliament House was opened in 1988. Nearby is the old Parliament House, which is now a museum.

Before Australia's Federation, the politicians of Melbourne and Sydney argued about which city should be the capital of the nation. It was decided that neither city would be; instead the Australian Capital Territory was declared on 1 January 1911, and the city of Canberra was founded in 1913.

Parliament House has 4500 rooms and is one of the largest buildings in the Southern Hemisphere.

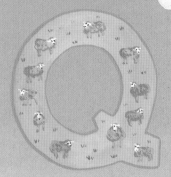

Qui Qui is a sheep station in Queensland. In Australia, there are more sheep than people.

The Royal Flying Doctor Service treats sick and injured people in the outback. The planes are also used as ambulances, flying patients to hospital.

Australia is the world's leading producer of wool.

The world's largest sheep and cattle station is in Australia. It covers an area of 6 million acres and is larger than the European country of Belgium.

A muster is a way of gathering cattle, sheep or horses. Working dogs run on the backs of sheep when mustering. Sometimes helicopters are used on large stations.

Many children in the outback don't go to school – school comes to them via School of the Air. In the past, children linked with their teachers by radio. Now they use satellite technology.

Jackaroos (male workers) and jillaroos (female workers) perform a range of jobs on cattle and sheep stations.

Rottnest Island (WA), or "Rotto" as it's known to the locals, is a short ferry ride off the west coast of Australia.

Secluded beaches and bays are famous for swimming, snorkelling, fishing and surfing.

The Basin is a natural swimming hole protected by a shallow reef a few steps from the beach.

Willem de Vlamingh, a Dutch explorer, visited the island in 1696. He mistook the quokkas, small marsupials living on the island, for giant rats and named the island "Rotte nest" (meaning rat's nest), which later became "Rottnest".

The Aboriginal name for Rottnest Island is *Wadjemup*, a Noongar word meaning "place across the water". The island is a place of sadness for Aboriginal people. Between 1838 and 1904 Rottnest served as a prison for Aboriginal men and boys.

Every year there is a 20-kilometre swimming race from the mainland across the Indian Ocean to the island.

You can't take your car to Rottnest so the best way to get around the island is by bicycle.

 **Sydney** (NSW) is home to Australia's best-known landmarks – the Harbour Bridge and the Opera House.

The Sydney Opera House, Australia's most iconic building, was designed by Danish architect Jørn Utzon. It took 16 years to build and was opened in 1973.

Sydney Opera House is located on Bennelong Point on the land of the Gadigal people. It was named after Bennelong, a man who worked to make peace between Aboriginal people and the first European settlers. The Aboriginal name for the point is *Tu-bow-gule*, meaning "meeting of the waters".

Paul Robeson was the first person to sing at the Sydney Opera House while it was being built. He sang "Ol' Man River" to the workers as they ate their lunch on the top of the scaffolding.

During a show featuring live chickens, a playful chicken fell off the Opera House stage and landed on a cellist's head. Shortly after, a net that had been tested to hold the weight of 70 chickens was installed above the orchestra pit.

Sydney Harbour Bridge is affectionately called the "Coat Hanger" because of its shape. You can climb 1437 steps to the top of the bridge.

The bridge took 8 years to build and was opened in 1932. The 485,000 square metres of steelwork is grey because there was no other colour available in such a large quantity.

The metal arch of the bridge rises and falls 18 centimetres when the temperature changes. The bridge has special hinges that retract and expand.

One way to see Sydney Harbour is by ferry. Circular Quay is the hub of the harbour; boats go to Taronga Zoo, Cockatoo Island and the famous voyage to Manly starts here.

Torres Strait Islands

are located off Australia's northernmost point, Cape York.

The Torres Strait is named after a Spanish captain, Luis Vaez de Torres, who sailed through the strait in 1606.

Torres Strait Islanders have strong cultural bonds with the sea and land that are kept alive through ceremonies where the Islanders wear bright costumes and a traditional feathered headdress called a *dari*.

There are at least 274 islands in the Torres Strait but only 17 are populated.

The Torres Strait was the first place in Australia where native title was recognised, acknowledging Indigenous people's rights to the land. Eddie "Koiki" Mabo, a Merriam man, led the fight for native title, and in 1992 the High Court of Australia acknowledged his people's traditional ownership of land on the island of Mer. It is commonly known as the Mabo decision.

Captain Bligh, of the HMS *Bounty*, named Tuesday, Wednesday, Thursday and Friday Islands after the days he spotted them.

Dugongs graze mostly on seagrass and are also called seacows. Australia has the last major dugong population in the world.

Sailors once thought dugongs were mermaids.

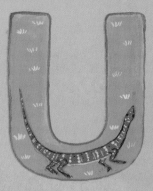

Uluru (NT) is one of the largest rocks in the world, reaching 9 kilometres around and standing 350 metres high.

The traditional owners of Uluru are the Yankunytjatjara and Pitjantjatjara people, locally known as Anangu.

More than two-thirds of the rock is hidden underground.

Dingoes do not bark, but they can purr and howl.

Perenties are the biggest lizards in Australia, reaching 2 metres or more in length.

Uluru is a sacred site. The traditional owners ask visitors to respect their law and not climb the rock.

Uluru gets its rusty-red colour from oxidised iron in the sandstone. But at sunrise or sunset it can appear to glow orange, a fiery red or even blue or violet.

Nearby are huge domes of rocks called *Kata-Tjuta* which means "many heads".

Valley of the Giants (WA) is in the Walpole-Nornalup National Park and is home to the rare red tingle trees.

The treetop walk climbs through the canopy of the forest to give visitors a bird's eye view.

An old tingle tree, affectionately known as "Grandma Tingle", is said to be over 400 years old.

The tingle trapdoor spider is the size of a pinhead. Although recently discovered, they have actually been around for thousands of years.

This area is known as *Kurrabup* by the Noongar people, the traditional owners of the land.

You can walk right through the middle of a giant tingle tree where the trunk has split during a bushfire.

Red tingle trees have the widest base of all gum trees with a girth of up to 24 metres and can grow up to 75 metres tall.

Western grey kangaroos, honey possums, bandicoots and a variety of parrots live in the forest.

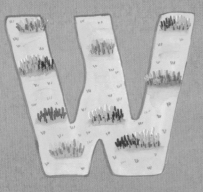

Walls of Jerusalem National Park

(Tas) got its name from the natural features that resemble the walls of the city of Jerusalem

The platypus has a bill like a duck, a tail like a beaver and swims with its eyes shut. The male platypus has deadly spurs. The females are one of the few mammals to lay eggs.

The Tasmanian devil can eat up to a third of its body weight in a single meal. Its jaw is so strong that it can gnaw through a metal trap.

Tasmania has some of the cleanest air and water in the world. The rainwater is so pure that it was shipped to the Seoul Olympic Games for Australian athletes to drink.

Many places within the park have biblical names such as Herod's Gate, Lake Salome, Damascus Gate and King David's Peak.

A pencil pine can live over 1200 years, but some Huon pines can live over 3000 years, making it Australia's oldest tree.

The extinct Tasmanian tiger (thylacine) looked like a large dog with stripes. It had a stiff tail and could open its mouth 120 degrees. Benjamin, the last known Tasmanian tiger, died in a Hobart zoo in 1936. Some people believe the thylacine may still survive in the Tasmanian wilderness.

A 4-hour hike from the park's entrance is the only way to reach this remote wilderness.

EXmouth (WA) is the gateway town to the Ningaloo Reef, one of the longest fringing reefs in the world.

Adult whale sharks can grow up to 12 metres long, weigh 20 tonnes and live for 60 to 100 years.

The name Ningaloo originated from an Aboriginal West Thalanyji, Jinigudira, Yinigudura and Yinkutura word, meaning "deep water".

Whale sharks are not actually whales but the biggest fish in the world. Many cultures believe they are good luck fish.

Yallingup (WA) is a coastal town famous for its beaches and limestone caves.

Yallingup is a Noongar Aboriginal word meaning "place of love".

Powerful breaks like Three Bears, Super Tubes and Rabbits are some of the best surfing spots in the world.

Nearby is Ngilgi Cave, named after an Aboriginal legend. It's a subterranean wonderland of crystal stalactites, stalagmites and shawl formations.

Taronga Zoo (NSW)

is home to thousands of animals from around the world as well as Australian native wildlife.

The Cammeraigal people are the traditional owners of the land where Taronga Zoo is located.

The echidna eats ants with its long sticky tongue and has a prickly coat similar to a porcupine.

Kookaburras are known for their call that sounds like a person laughing.

Koalas are only active for about 4 hours of the day and spend the rest of their time sleeping. They're sometimes called bears because they look like teddy bears.

Red kangaroos can travel as fast as 65 kilometres per hour and can leap 8 metres in a single bound.

Female kangaroos have pouches where their young, called joeys, are raised until they can survive outside the pouch.

Wombats have square poo. Sometimes they sleep on their backs with all four feet sticking straight up in the air.

Emus can grow to 2 metres tall. They cannot fly but are fast runners. The male builds the nest and sits on the green eggs for 7 to 8 weeks, never leaving the nest the entire time.

For Mark, who showed me the country I now call home. FL

First published in 2015
by Walker Books Australia Pty Ltd
Locked Bag 22, Newtown
NSW 2042 Australia
www.walkerbooks.com.au

National Library of Australia Cataloguing-in-Publication entry:
Lessac, Frané, author, illustrator.
A is for Australia/author/illustrator Frané Lessac.
ISBN: 978 1 922179 76 0 (hardback)
For children.
Subjects: Australia – Juvenile literature.
994

The illustrations for this book were created with gouache on arches paper
Typeset in Futura Book
Printed and bound in China

7 9 10 8 6